Citizenship

Being Fair

Cassie Mayer

Heinemann Library
Chicago, Illinois

© 2008 Heinemann Library
a division of Reed Elsevier Inc.
Chicago, Illinois

Customer Service 888-454-2279
Visit our website at www.heinemannraintree.com

Designed by Joanna Hinton-Malivoire
Illustrated by Mark Beech
Printed and bound in China by South China Printing Co. Ltd.

11 10 09 08 07
10 9 8 7 6 5 4 3 2 1

The Library of Congress has cataloged the first edition of this book as follows:
Mayer, Cassie.
  Being fair / Cassie Mayer.
     p. cm. -- (Citizenship)
  Includes bibliographical references and index.
  ISBN 978-1-4034-9483-2 (hc) -- ISBN 978-1-4034-9491-7 (pbk.) 1. Fairness--Juvenile literature. I. Title.
  BJ1533.F2M39 2007
  179'.9--dc22
                                        2006039378

Contents

Being fair means thinking of
other people.

Being fair means treating
people well.

When you share your toys ...

you are being fair.

When you wait your turn …

you are being fair.

When you give someone else
a turn ...

you are being fair.

When you share a snack
with friends ...

you are being fair.

When you ask others to join in ...

you are being fair.

When you let others choose what
to play ...

you are being fair.

When you think of how
others feel ...

you are being fair.

Being fair is important.

How can you be fair?

Activity

How is this child being fair?

Picture Glossary

fair agreeable for everyone

share to let someone else use what you have; to give someone else a part of what you have

Index

Note to Parents and Teachers
Each book in this series shows examples of behavior that demonstrate good citizenship. Take time to discuss each illustration and ask children to identify the fair behavior shown. Use the question on page 21 to ask students how they can be fair in their own lives.

The text has been chosen with the advice of a literacy expert to enable beginning readers success while reading independently or with moderate support. You can support children's nonfiction literacy skills by helping them use the table of contents, picture glossary, and index.